A little Muse

Max Todes

BookLeaf Publishing
India | USA | UK

Presentation by *BookLeaf Publishing*

Web: www.bookleafpub.com

E-mail: info@bookleafpub.com

ISBN: 978-93-5744-349-4

First edition 2022

ACKNOWLEDGEMENT

I would like to thank my parents and sister. The former for my first little brown notebook to write poems in, and the latter for not laughing to hard when I read from said book.

Forlorn

Forlorn the sea, still weeps the waves
Who gently sob in cragish graves
Their frothy tears seep into sand
And crashing cries aren't hear on land.

Forlorn the sea, still weeps the shore
On which rests the lapis moor
And without shores a wave can't be
For waves can't fall on open sea.

Forlorn the sea, still weeps the stars
For dashing waves leave slashing scars
That numbing saline never heals
Nor sunny rays the truth reveals.

Rawls

2

Darkness Rawls yet summer shines for thee
Hope for sweet melody revolts not nor lingers
long on laurels
For in thy shining eyes and grace,
It finds forevermore its resting place

The soul of such a smile
Does not by nature's countenance
Seek wanton form of statues ire

So rests beneath the duplets that adorn thy face
And seeks to softly decorate each warm embrace

Rawls II

Darkness Rawls as the night slowly crawls
Through crippled fabric and glitter,
The hum and slow of the pitter of day,
Suspends of the clouds and rain-
and all who laugh at never again

Darkness Rawls as the lilacs display
The feathers of faeries as seen in the day
The soft gentle ripples in droplets and leethes
In nature demeaned like the birds and the trees

It is they who laugh and rise with the hills
The mountains, the sea and the sky as it fills
With triplets of birdsong and petals of acorn
And images of chaos that swirl and deride
The type of suspicion they often surmise...

The beauty is clear to all that can see
But never quite clear to the writer in me.

Prussia Cove

Incandescent blue shines bright
With tips of frothy mareish white-

Yet storied winds and lighting
Ever rages frightening-

In waves and crashes such resound
In caves and beachy mounds-

That lies the epic story tells
Of funeral shrouds and wedding bells-

Oft a moment on the hills
In sullen walls and windowsills-

Is made for all and all who see
In Cornwall love is made for thee

Strings, Percussion and Celesta

In finished lines, in absence draws
Begins the fragile message, trawls-
Between the lines, adjacent tones
An angular figure lulls and roams

In one voice it utters still
A music that by nature will-
tread once more a trodden path…

Such soft undulations have already been
Discordant, raging with glorious sheen

Its roots shall grow, and it must rise
Amassing lines towards the skies
But built not out of bable fame
For surely they don't speak the same…

Yet a larger structure drives
A logic-apt, before our eyes
One I profess I could not hear
But yet exists in golden spheres

In finished lines in absence drawn
Behold a might structure born
That creates these lines and tone
An alchemic structure glorious shown.

Ellipse

Never ending straight-knit lines
Upon the paper oft inclines
A languid shape, curvaceous sprawls
Around a central orbit pulls

A shape unseen, such is the eye
For such infinity would be a lie
Thus what it is, in mind alone
A graphite simulacrum clone

The Chapel

The chapel
The rusty hinges on the door,
The towering ceiling up above,
And underneath the dusty floor,
The cobwebs hanging all around,
Crack down the chapel goes in whole burnt to a
little crisp.

The Arch

Towering above the ground below,
Arching up in the sky.
On stone on stone it stands alone in the misty
quiet courtyard.
It stands to the very last of days,
Even in the summer with the sun's golden rays,
Even in the winter when the waves pound on the
shore, It stands still and sturdy as ever as before.

Signs

I look upon this scruffy page
And as I write this new delight
Of songful shapes the lines create
Of morish sounds and palpable rhymes
These often-curious cryptic signs
Invasive in my head they sound
In such a way I can't confound

Max

The stillness that surrounds my eyes,
Can often catch me by surprise
And if something beyond it calls
A patient moment quickly falls –

Beyond my mind, and from my eye
Escapes the image of the sky
For now I know I'll never see
The horrid looks they give to me

And even then, I feel them stare
A look, a glance, a wince, a glare
But for the laugh they need not see,
But simply listen for brayed top C's.

Loss

The sun is dying once again,
The Sky is wet with tears,
The tears of many a mother's love,
For a child lost so dear.

And the sky is red with blood,
Of many a war with greed and strife,
And soldiers lying in the trench,
The children on a crowded bench.

The sky is weeping, for it knows,
That the lovely little rose,
Will die like the sun that goeth down,
And darkness falleth all around.

But once again there will be light,
For evil, darkness in the fight,
Will not prevail to our delight.

So then again the sun will rise,
The crowning glory of our skies,
But all good reigns must come and go,

And so.

The sun is dying once again,
The sky has dropped a tear,
A tear to cleanse the saddening weight, Over
many a year.

Others

I've always wondered why I see –
Things smaller, far away from me
Indeed, I've looked upon a house
And thought it merely just a mouse

And so I often look right at –
Myself and wonder if I sat
Some distance from where all I saw
Is some silhouette stood at the door

Could I tell just from his face
The life he leads and keeps a pace
Could I see past by his smile
Would that stay with me a while?

Bella

Of what I cannot conceive, I can only wonder
Of what I cannot believe, I must surely cast
asunder.
For both cannot be entertained
Far from that nothing can be gained

But rather look tomorrow's dawn
Not back at loves of friendships worn
So leave to go, not long to stay
And those with whom the sunny day-

Has long been spent for summers past
But winter soon must come at last-

Do not mistake its frosty chill
The newness in its snowy frill
Though changed and blank the world may be
A fresh new canvas lacking me…

With warmth and time, the chill will fade
With those you meet, with friends you've made
And happy me whose joy to see
The glorious person you've come to be

Sunset

The sun in its cradle hung low in the sky,
Its beautiful rays beginning to die.
Across silky dark waters the suns final rays,
Leapt up and down on its last lulling waves.

The sea now gold from the light of the heavens,
Wept and danced as the night slowly beckoned.

From the flawless blue canvas a myriad of stars,
no hint of the sunset just a glint of bright Mars.

With the stars and the spheres filling the sky,
And the moon on the horizon just starting to
fly…

One moment of silence,
A passing of thought,
A few of the things,
That this sunset had brought.

The handful of people to see such a sight,
Went home and dreamt and slept well that night.

For such was the beauty of the spheres they had
seen,

They wondered in the morning if it had been but
a dream.

Dom

There once was a man named Dom
Whose limericks were awfully long
He whipped them up quick
And although they were slick
They were never particularly strong

A Kiwi

Unattractive, like barnacles on a rock in the
blistering sun,
Spider legs,
Sporadic hairs protruding
Rough and coarse,

Underneath, a closer look,
Green the purest shade,
Not plentiful in that great haze

Its skin, callous in nature,
Brown and unforgiving to the eye,
And yet it hides such sustenance
Becomes untoward of its appearance, but at least
it tries…

But as you smell the wafting of that tangy whiff,
So sweet it makes the air,
A simple piece of paradise,
A pity it's so rare,

But there are people who can't see,
the beauty in the things that be,

for so conceited they've become,
that flattery is overdone

And through their glasses of tinted rose,
Such imperfections oft imposed...

Blue

Why do I adore you so
A precious shade of arctic glow
Of sunny skies and wanton breeze
Of waters deep where darkness flees

I live in souls with such a smile
That nods and stays with you awhile.

Shapes not sounds

I wonder if I could ever see
Words as shapes not heard as sound
Not like they often come to me
But in the form that they were found

I wonder if words might collect before-
Me as I face the paper and draw
These rabid scratches
Of lines and like
Of florid elephantine strikes

Of droplets collected before the ground-
A promise not delivered thus unbroken sand
Of music that rounds in the mind not the ear
can only but help but naturally cohere

It cannot repeat or occur quite alike
for promotion of difference is only in sight
though one can't assume to order our world
by such passive logic that's never unfurled

Indeed if I'm immanent then how could I know
of anything more than of white lilting snow

of bangeries tickeld and wortels surround

with bright bandyrickles – yet still they are
sounds

I wonder if I could ever see
Words as shapes not heard as sound
Not like they often come to me
But in the form that they were found

The end of Time

On flittered wings and gleaming eyes
With shrieking songs above me flies

A bird that rests upon the tree
Rests, but never hast to be.

For though it seeks a sheltered shore
It's not a place it's forced to moor

The branches barbed with only thorns
And death of elders only morns-

As I watched the bird in flight
A picture still in single sight-

I wonder how it came to be
That these birds might sing free
A subtle ache within my soul
Of tuneful fragments never whole

For my feet are on the ground
And all I can is shriek for sound

I cannot reach their lofty heights
I cannot soar above those kites

But mindlessly it tears the soul
Away from that which makes it whole

And thrust away from temporal grasp
To rest and sing with birds at last.